INDIGENOUS BIOGRAPHIES

# Joy Harjo

## Poet Laureate

FOCUS READERS BEACON

by Katrina M. Phillips

www.focusreaders.com



Focus Readers is distributed by North Star Editions:
sales@northstareditions.com | 888-417-0195

Produced for Focus Readers by Red Line Editorial.

Photographs ©: Shawn Miller/Library of Congress, cover, 1, 4, 7, 29; Shutterstock Images, 8, 17, 22; National Portrait Gallery/Smithsonian Institution, 10; John Prieto/The Denver Post/Getty Images, 13; David Butow/Corbis Historical/Getty Images, 14; iStockphoto, 18; Russell Contreras/AP Images, 21; Paul Abdoo/MPI/Archive Photos/Getty Images, 25; Lauren Petracca/AP Images, 27

**Library of Congress Cataloging-in-Publication Data**
Names: Phillips, Katrina M., author.
Title: Joy Harjo: poet laureate / by Katrina M. Phillips.
Description: Mendota Heights, MN: Focus Readers, [2026] | Series: Indigenous biographies | Includes index. | Audience: Grades 2-3
Identifiers: LCCN 2025012045 (print) | LCCN 2025012046 (ebook) | ISBN 9798889985013 (hardcover) | ISBN 9798889986553 (paperback) | ISBN 9798889985648 (pdf) | ISBN 9798889985334 (ebook)
Subjects: LCSH: Harjo, Joy--Juvenile literature. | Indian poets--Biography--Juvenile literature. | Poets laureate--Biography--Juvenile literature. | Creek Indians--Biography--Juvenile literature. | LCGFT: Literature. | Biographies.
Classification: LCC PS3558.A62423 Z84 2026 (print) | LCC PS3558.A62423 (ebook) | DDC 811/.54 [B]--dc23/eng/20250418
LC record available at https://lccn.loc.gov/2025012045
LC ebook record available at https://lccn.loc.gov/2025012046

Printed in the United States of America
Mankato, MN
012026

## About the Author

Dr. Katrina M. Phillips (Red Cliff Ojibwe) is a writer, researcher, and history professor. She's written several children's books about Native histories and cultures, including *Indigenous Peoples' Day* and *I Am on Indigenous Land*. She and her husband live in Minnesota with their two sons and their goofy dog.

# Table of Contents

CHAPTER 1

# Making History

In 2019, writer Joy Harjo made history. She was named poet laureate of the United States. She was the first **Indigenous** person to serve in the role. A poet laureate acts as the nation's official poet.

**Joy Harjo was the first person from Oklahoma to be named poet laureate.**

This person also helps the public **appreciate** poetry.

A poet laureate serves from September to April. Most serve two terms. But Harjo was chosen for a third term. She was only the second person to earn that honor. She served from 2019 to 2022.

## Did You Know?

Harjo was the 23rd poet laureate in US history.

In 2022, Harjo held a poetry class for Native writers.

Harjo did many things as poet laureate. She brought attention to Indigenous poetry. She broke **stereotypes** of Indigenous peoples. She brought Indigenous writers together. And she helped them share their stories.

CHAPTER 2

# Growing Up Muscogee

Joy Harjo was born in Tulsa, Oklahoma, on May 9, 1951. Her father was a **citizen** of the Muscogee (Creek) Nation. Joy came from a family of respected Muscogee warriors and leaders.

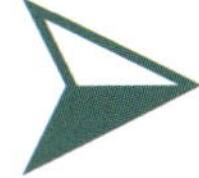

**In the 1950s, more than 180,000 people lived in Tulsa, Oklahoma.**

**Joy's ancestor was Menawa. He led the Muscogee in a key battle.**

One of her **ancestors** fought against the United States in the Red Stick War (1813–1814). This is also known as the Creek War. Some Muscogee people wanted to fight back against American settlement. They were known as the Red Sticks.

Joy grew up surrounded by art and music. Her mother wrote songs. She loved poetry. Sometimes she played with a band. Joy's aunt and grandmother were artists.

## Did You Know?

**Joy wrote her first poem when she was in eighth grade. As a child, one of her favorite poets was Emily Dickinson.**

Her grandmother's paintings filled the walls of Joy's childhood home.

However, her childhood was not always easy. Joy did not always feel safe at home. She turned to painting. This helped her share her thoughts and feelings. She took acting classes, too.

Joy moved when she was 16 years old. She went to New Mexico. She began attending the Institute of American Indian Arts (IAIA). This high school started in 1962. Native

**Joy's advisor at the IAIA was Quapaw–Cherokee music composer Louis W. Ballard.**

students from across the country went to IAIA. Many of them became famous artists, musicians, writers, and poets.

CHAPTER 3

# Finding Her Voice

Joy Harjo went to IAIA to be a painter. But she was inspired by many people she met in school. She joined a drama group and a dance group. Joy also wrote songs for a rock band.

**Indigenous painter Fritz Scholder taught art at IAIA when Joy Harjo was a student.**

The band was made up of all Indigenous musicians.

Joy finished high school in 1968. Afterward, she enrolled at the University of New Mexico. She planned to study medicine there. Then she switched to art.

Harjo had never known anyone who was a poet or a writer. But that changed in college. Many poets visited and read their work. Harjo loved it. She also became involved in Native **activism**.

**The University of New Mexico is in Albuquerque, New Mexico.**

This work inspired her to start writing poetry. Soon, she decided to study creative writing.

Harjo released her first book in 1975. It was called *The Last Song*.

**One poem in Harjo's 1975 book featured the Manzano Mountains in New Mexico.**

In these poems, Harjo wrote about New Mexico and Oklahoma. She wrote about the experiences of Native people in the past and the present.

Harjo finished college the next year. Then she earned a master's degree in poetry at the Iowa Writers' Workshop. Harjo continued to publish poetry. She also began teaching. She taught at IAIA. And she taught at colleges in Arizona, Colorado, and New Mexico.

## Did You Know?

**Harjo has often included historical events in her writing. One example is the Trail of Tears.**

TOPIC SPOTLIGHT

# Indigenous Authors

Native people have always told stories. For example, Ojibwe writer William Whipple Warren lived in the 1800s. He became known for his history of the Ojibwe people. Charles Eastman was another Native writer. He wrote books and gave talks around the United States.

A new movement of Native writers began in the 1960s. These writers included Joy Harjo. They also included N. Scott Momaday, James Welch, and Louise Erdrich. They published novels, **memoirs**, poetry, and nonfiction pieces. They inspired many future Native authors.

A novel by Kiowa writer N. Scott Momaday won the Pulitzer Prize in 1969. That is one of the top writing awards in the United States.

CHAPTER 4

# A Life in Writing

Joy Harjo has written many poems and books of poetry. She has written memoirs. She's also written children's books, screenplays, and stage plays.

**In 1989, Joy Harjo released a book that had both poems and photos. It featured many parts of the Southwest, including Shiprock.**

One of Harjo's most famous pieces is called "She Had Some Horses." The poem repeats "She had horses" at the beginning of most lines. It uses many opposites, such as love and hate. The poem expresses the pain and joy of being a Native woman.

Harjo also became known as a musician. She learned to play the saxophone when she was 40 years old. She took up the flute, too. Harjo started playing music for audiences

Harjo learned multiple kinds of saxophone, including the soprano saxophone.

in the early 1990s. She performed around the world. She also released several albums.

Harjo earned many awards in the 2020s. She became part of the National Women's Hall of Fame. She was given the lifetime achievement award from the National Arts Awards. Harjo also received the National Humanities Medal. This award is given to people who have

## Did You Know?

**Harjo released a new book in 2025. It explored how to deal with the pain of losing someone.**

**Harjo (left) appears with other new members of the National Women's Hall of Fame in 2022.**

had an effect on others through history or **literature**.

Harjo continued writing. She kept speaking out as well. She used her music and poetry to tell stories about Native histories and Native futures.

# Focus Questions

*Write your answers on a separate piece of paper.*

1. Write a letter to a friend about Joy Harjo's life.
2. What would you like to write a poem about? Why?
3. When did Harjo release her first book of poems?
   - **A.** 1968
   - **B.** 1975
   - **C.** 2019
4. Why might Harjo have turned to writing poetry later in college?
   - **A.** She tried to avoid poetry for as long as possible.
   - **B.** Her family did not like the arts very much.
   - **C.** She started meeting people who were writers.

**5.** What does **enrolled** mean in this sentence?

*Joy finished high school in 1968. Afterward, she* ***enrolled*** *at the University of New Mexico. She planned to study medicine there.*

**A.** stopped learning new things
**B.** signed up for a school
**C.** did well on a difficult test

**6.** What does **expresses** mean in this sentence?

*It uses many opposites, such as love and hate. The poem* ***expresses*** *the pain and joy of being a Native woman.*

**A.** talks about
**B.** opposes
**C.** hides

*Answer key on page 32.*

# Glossary

**activism**
Actions to make social or political changes.

**ancestors**
Family members from the past.

**appreciate**
To recognize the importance of something.

**citizen**
A person who is a legal member of a certain nation.

**Indigenous**
Native to a region, or belonging to ancestors who lived in a region before colonists arrived.

**literature**
Written work that is seen as a piece of art.

**memoirs**
Book or essays that tell about people's lives and memories.

**stereotypes**
Overly simple and harmful ideas of how all members of a certain group are.

**Trail of Tears**
The forced removal of thousands of Native people from their homelands in the 1800s.

# To Learn More

## BOOKS

Grand, Keely. *Troublemakers and Superpowers: 29 Stories of People Who Turned Childhood Struggles into Strengths*. Sasquatch Books, 2023.

Harjo, Joy. *For a Girl Becoming*. Norton Young Readers, 2025.

Harjo, Joy. *Remember*. Penguin Random House, 2023.

## NOTE TO EDUCATORS

Visit **www.focusreaders.com** to find links and resources related to this title.

# Index



**Answer Key:** 1. Answers will vary; 2. Answers will vary; 3. B; 4. C; 5. B; 6. A